CONCERT ARABESQUES

on motifs by Johann Strauss

("By the Beautiful Blue Danube")

arranged by Andrei Schulz-Evler

ED 4115

ISBN 978-0-634-00862-7

G. SCHIRMER, Inc.

DISTRIBUTED BY
HAL•LEONARD®
CORPORATION
7777 W. BLUEMOUND RD. P.O. BOX 13819 MILWAUKEE, WI 53213

CONCERT ARABESQUES
on motifs by Johann Strauss
("By the Beautiful Blue Danube")

Edited and fingered by
Paolo Gallico

Andrei Schulz–Evler

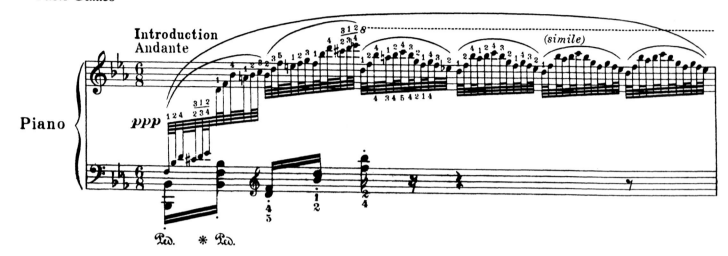

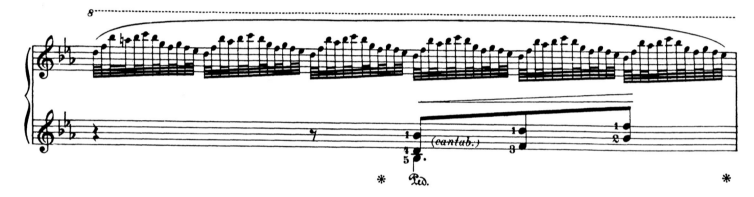

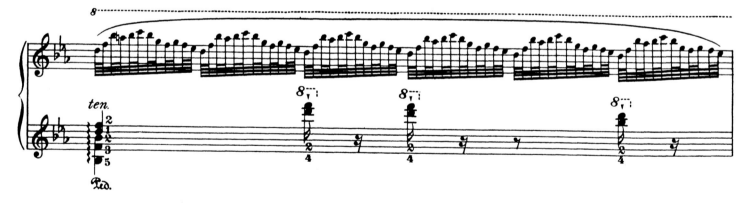

19236 r x

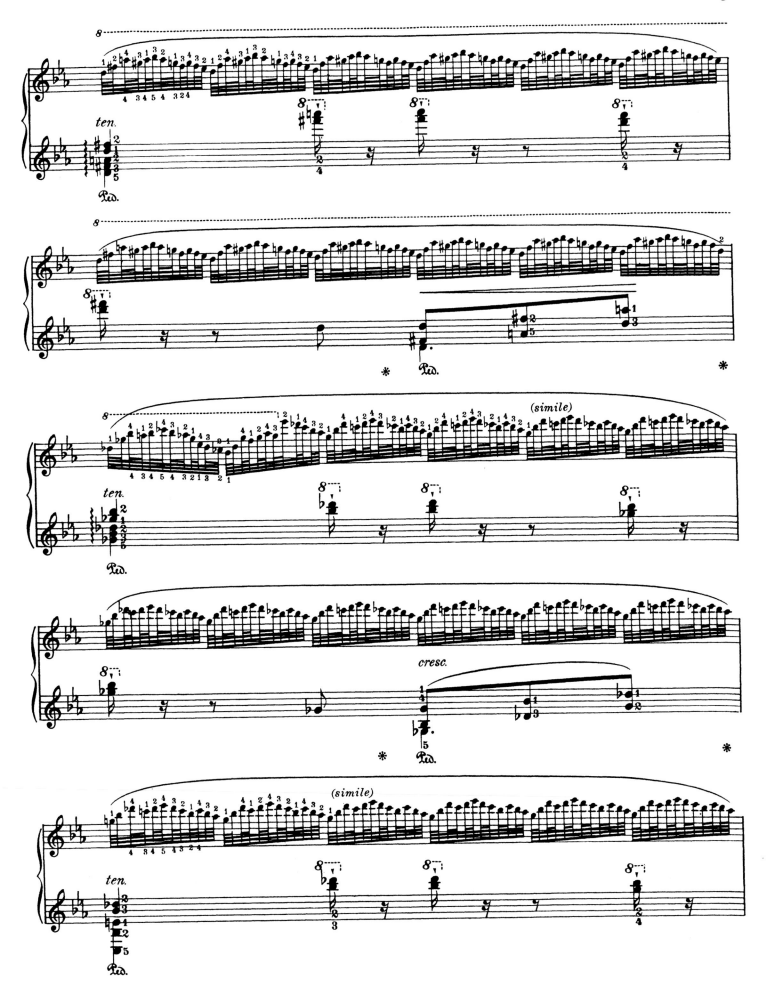

4

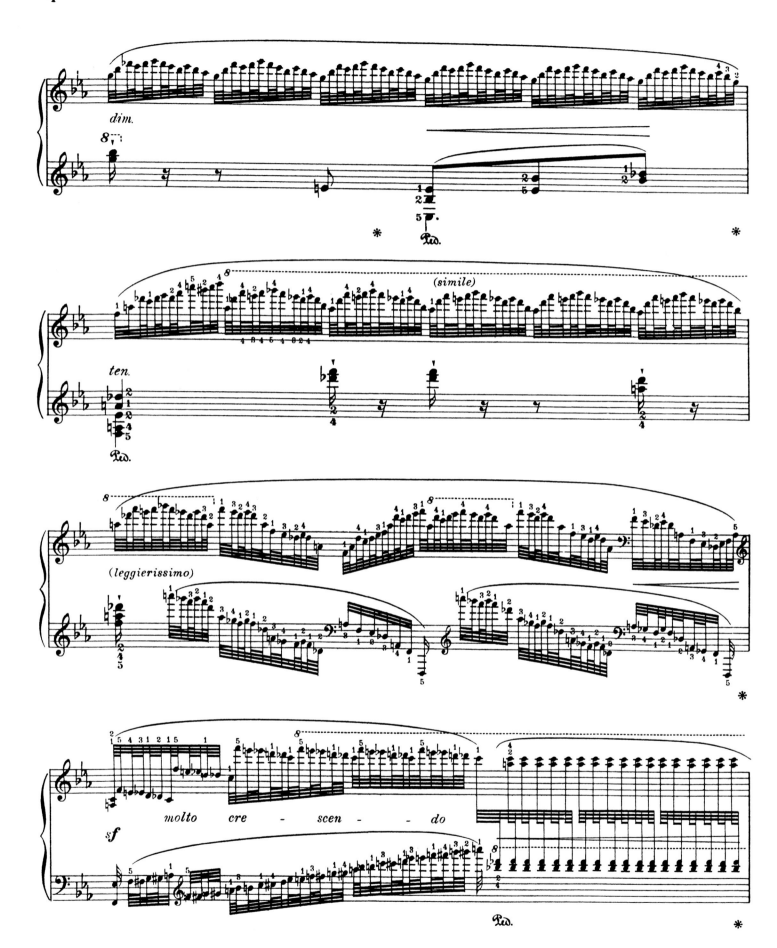

Tempo di Valse

a) Strike lower B with both hands.

19236

Valse No. 1

Valse № 2

Valse № 3

11

Valse Nº 4

Valse № 5 et Coda

0-73999-44032-4

0 73999 44032 4

HL50483612

G. SCHIRMER, Inc.

DISTRIBUTED BY

U.S. $8.99

ISBN 978-0-634-00862-7

9 780634 008627

50899